Table of Contents

Rourke
Educational Media
A Division of
Carson Dellosa Education
rourkeeducationalmedia.com

Can you find these words?

dreidel

gifts

latkes

menorah

We Celebrate Hanukkah!

Hanukkah lasts for eight winter days.

3

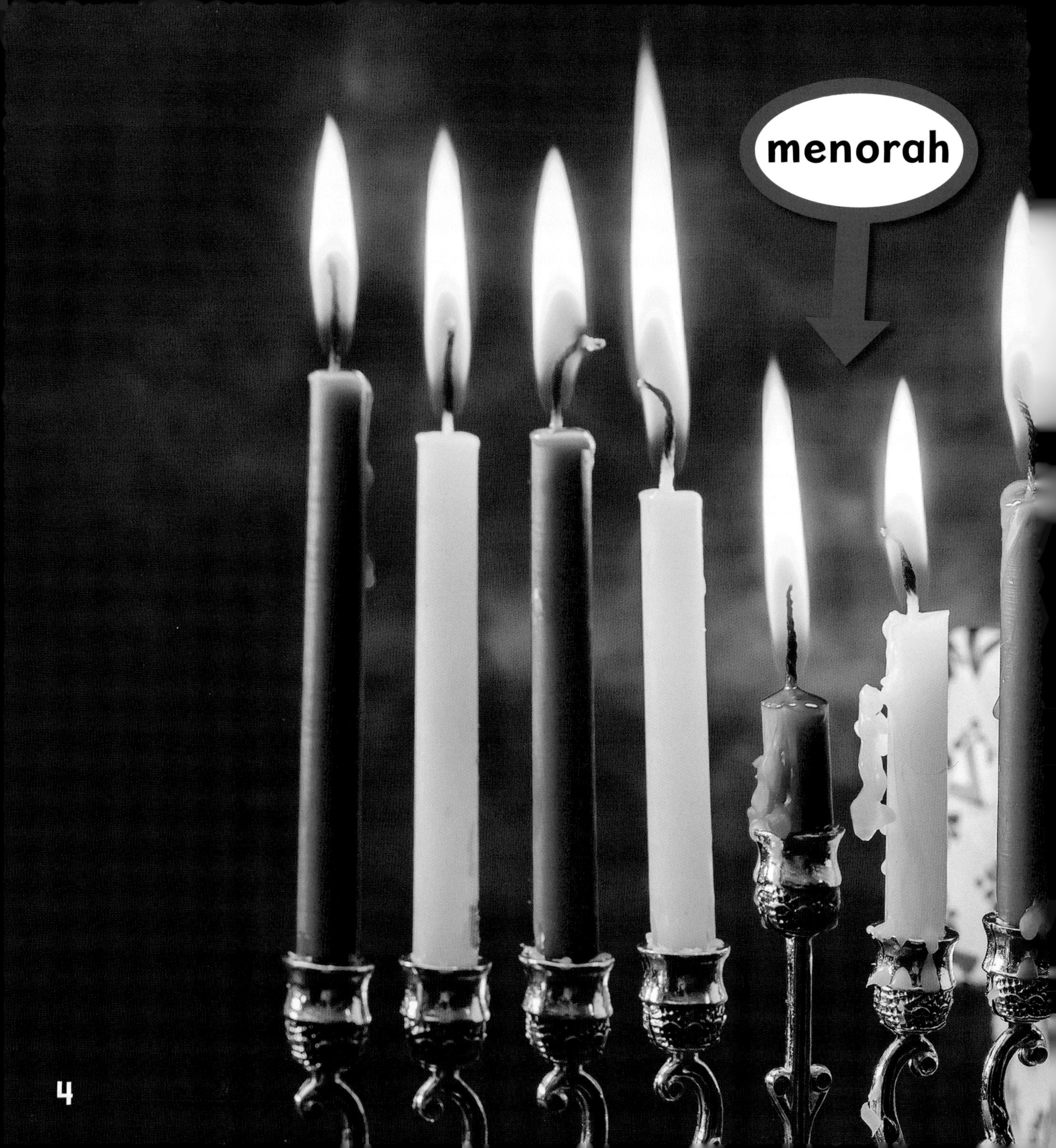
menorah

Let's light the **menorah.**

Let's sing!

Remember the stories of the Jewish people.

gifts

Let's open presents!

Families trade **gifts** each night.

Let's spin the **dreidel**.

Play for prizes!

dreidel

11

Let's eat **latkes** and jelly doughnuts.

latkes

Yum!

Did you find these words?

Let's spin the **dreidel**.

Families trade **gifts** each night.

Let's eat **latkes** and jelly doughnuts.

Let's light the **menorah**.

14

Photo Glossary

 **dreidel** (DRAY-duhl): A four-sided toy marked with Hebrew letters and spun like a top.

 **gifts** (gifts): Items given as presents.

 **latkes** (LAHT-kuhs): Potato pancakes.

 **menorah** (muh-NOR-uh): A candleholder that holds nine candles and is used during Hanukkah.

Index

About the Author

Lisa Jackson is a writer from Columbus, Ohio. She likes to ride her bike and collect pennies. Her favorite holiday is the one that is coming up next!

www.rourkeeducationalmedia.com

PHOTO CREDITS: Cover: ©By Arina P Habich; Pg 2, 10, 14, 15 ©kali9; Pg 2, 13, 14, 15 ©a_namenko; Pg 2, 4, 14, 15 ©photovs; Pg 2, 9, 14, 15 ©photovs; Pg 3 ©CatLane; Pg 6 ©pushlama

Edited by: Keli Sipperley
Cover and interior design by: Kathy Walsh

Library of Congress PCN Data
Hanukkah / Lisa Jackson
(Holidays Around the World)
ISBN 978-1-73160-575-7 (hard cover)(alk. paper)
ISBN 978-1-73160-450-7 (soft cover)
ISBN 978-1-73160-624-2 (e-Book)
ISBN 978-1-73160-687-7 (ePub)
Library of Congress Control Number: 2018967332

Printed in the United States of America,
North Mankato, Minnesota